A PATHWAY TO
EMOTIONAL SOBRIETY
AND HOW TO GET IT

The Life Changing Magic of
Feeling the Moment and Being Yourself

GRANDMASTER
Craig Hutson

A Pathway To Emotional Sobriety and How To Get It
The Life Changing Magic of Feeling the Moment and Being Yourself

© 2021 Craig Hutson. All rights reserved.

No part of this book may be reproduced or transmitted in any form or by any means, electronic or mechanical, including but not limited to: photocopying, recording, or by any information storage retrieval system without the written permission of the publisher, except for the inclusion of brief quotations in a review.

Editor: Julie Escobar, Speaker's Choice Consulting
Cover Design and Interior Layout: Kendra Cagle, 5 Lakes Design

Library of Congress Control Number: 2020951682

ISBN:
978-1-7360764-0-8 (paperback)
978-1-7360764-1-5 (Kindle)
978-1-7360764-2-2 (ePub)

Grandmaster Craig Hutson
www.DragonKido.com

Disclaimer:
The information in this book is for personal enlightenment. It is not meant to treat, diagnose or be a substitute for professional medical advice. Though it is presented in good faith, neither the author nor the publisher can assume responsibility or liability for any results, direct or consequential, from the experiment or practical application of this information.

DEDICATION

This book is dedicated to those in recovery who are searching for a new and more in-depth experience in self-examination and personal growth. To those who dare to examine their character traits to grow in understanding and wisdom and thereby achieve and experience emotional sobriety-as a new and enduring standard of being in their life. To the many therapists, counselors, and sponsors of the self-help groups across the nation.

TABLE OF CONTENTS

Preface i

Chapter 1 | The Letter. 1

Chapter 2 | Authenticity 7

Chapter 3 | The Ideology of Emotional Intelligence 11

Chapter 4 | The Big Six. 25

Chapter 5 | The Fix for Defects of Character. 37

Chapter 6 | Seven Deadly Sins & Corresponding Virtues 41

Chapter 7 | The Seventh Step 57

Chapter 8 | Transforming our Feelings into Words 61

Chapter 9 | Words That Heal 63

Chapter 10 | Power Patterns in Human Attitudes. 67

Chapter 11 | The Power of Affirmations. 71

Chapter 12 | Character Traits. 75

About the Author. 85

Sources Cited 87

PREFACE

I wrote this book to help improve the quality of understanding of the Big Book of Alcoholics Anonymous for people in recovery and to give a broader view of Steps Six and Seven. What I've learned is how incredibly vital it is to develop a different point of view. The notion that we can say a prayer and then forget about our responsibility to work on change that is essential to growth – both in recovery and as a human being is misguided.

With perspective and emotional sobriety, prayer is all most people think they need to do. That's a misconception. I am very concerned with people misunderstanding the meaning of the two Steps Six and Seven in The Big Book of Alcoholics Anonymous. Many books have been written to assist individuals in deepening their understanding of how to live with their feelings. I hope that the ideas which follow in this book can be extremely beneficial in giving you the direction you need to experience a deeper understanding of yourself and the personal growth you want.

After decades of practice, I understand the value of Emotional Sobriety and the overwhelming need for words that heal and affirm. Affirmations are crucial to re-scripting our lives. Developing a vocabulary of words that can help us improve can make for a more productive and purposeful journey. One of the things that change within us is the ability to discover that we can change irrational thinking into healthy rational thought.

Patience with ourselves is one of the greatest assets we can have. As a Martial Artist and Mentor, believing in those that have come before us and trusting their ability to teach us is imperative.

As stated in **www.Dragonkido.com**,

"Martial arts are not about fighting, but about how one lives."

LET'S SEE IF WE CAN'T
inspire some change for you.

CHAPTER ONE

THE LETTER

As we begin to explore change, let's first look at the significance of A.A.'s founder, Bill Wilson's letter, written in 1958 and how it applies to those in recovery today. My understanding is that this letter was written to encourage the people that had been around A.A. for some time, "the Old Timers," as we're frequently referred to, to share their experiences and teach newcomers how to grow emotionally by using the steps of A.A.

Later in this book, I'll share more about what the letter is asking us to do. Please realize that there are only a few snippets from the letter Bill wrote. These small excerpts could jump out at you and give you some direction. Each fragment has a few keywords in it that I hope will provide you with some insight. Words such as *spearhead, humility, adolescent urges, dependence, every ounce of will, my stability,* and lastly, *at the root of it*—are a few words you may see as essential to think about.

LET'S BREAKDOWN SOME OF THE MOST CRITICAL SEGMENTS FROM "THE NEXT FRONTIER: EMOTIONAL SOBRIETY," BY BILL WILSON:

As stated from www.silkworth.net, Bill W. said, "I think that many oldsters who have put our A.A. 'booze cure' to severe but successful tests still find they often lack emotional sobriety. Perhaps they will be the spearhead for the next major development in A.A., the development of much more real maturity and balance (which is to say, humility) in our relations with ourselves, with our fellowship, and with God.

Those adolescent urges that so many of us have for top approval, perfect security, and perfect romance urges quite appropriate to age seventeen – prove to be an impossible way of life when we are at age forty-seven or fifty-seven."

~ 2 ~

One critical thought to be addressed here first is that there is no cure for alcoholism. The notion of a booze cure does not exist. That being said, the one and most crucial factor is figuring out for ourselves how we can change and grow past old ideas. We need to develop a balance within ourselves that helps us integrate a new way of thinking that will help us mature. The first couple of paragraphs that Bill W. talked about in his letter is what this book is primarily talking about.

As an adult, I discovered the genuine value of integrating what I've learned from the world of Martial Arts into my sobriety practice and how important it is to actively practice words like **patience, perseverance, indomitable spirit,** and **self-control.** In doing so, I have grown my willingness and ability to stop blaming how I feel about other people's treatment of me. What I learned from practicing reasonable and practical words helped me to develop new ways to experience how I approach different situations.

The thought that comes to me is there is a technical way of saying this in the world of physiology, and that is "Psycho-Social Physiological Experience."

As you continue reading, you will better understand that the idea of depending on other people to measure and validate our self-worth and feel good about ourselves is faulty. In practicing martial arts and managing my thoughts and emotions when in the ring, I realized I had to protect myself from those individuals I was practicing against. I needed to tap into what my teacher was telling me about what to do and how to feel. For example, I once was fighting someone who kicked me in the head, and my teacher explained to me that person should control himself, but he wouldn't. Then my teacher told me to block the kick and learn excellent blocking skills—moments like that that taught me about HUMILITY.

As noted on Dr.Silkworth.net, Bill W. continued to state, "It then dawned on me that my fundamental flaw had always been dependence – almost absolute dependence – on people or circumstances to supply me with the feelings I craved, such as prestige, acknowledgment, security, and acceptance. Failing to get these things according to my perfectionist dreams and specifications, I fought for them. And when defeat came, so did my depression."

Depression was just the start. Feelings such as anger, disappointment, fear, frustration – also all reared their ugly heads. Learning to identify the opposite of each of those feelings, and practice the affirmations of those was, for me, the key to change. To experience the difference and increase my self-confidence, I had to exert a tremendous amount of willpower to practice positivity.

I found I had to use every ounce of will and action to cut off these faulty emotional dependencies upon people, upon A.A., and upon any external circumstances.

AS BILL W. MENTIONS IN HIS LETTER, HE HAD TO EXERT EVERY OUNCE OF WILL TO CHANGE. IT DOESN'T MATTER IF YOU'RE AN ALCOHOLIC OR NOT; CHANGE IS A CHOICE OF THE WILL.

Found from Dr. Silkworth.net, Bill W. continued to state, "In the first six months of my sobriety, I worked hard with many alcoholics. Not one responded. Yet this work kept me sober. It wasn't a question of those alcoholics giving me anything. My stability came out of trying to give, not out of demanding that I receive.

"Thus, I think that's what works with emotional sobriety. If we examine every disturbance we have, great or small, we will find, at the root of it, some unhealthy dependence and its consequent unhealthy demand."

In the following chapters, I will list some commonly expressed feelings used by individuals in self-help and recovery programs such as Alcoholics Anonymous, Narcotics Anonymous, and Emotions Anonymous. To learn how to discriminate between feeling powerful or sad is how we learn to practice distinguishing ourselves from others. These feelings will help you understand the most expressed emotions in their varying degrees of strength.

Most people in the martial arts are often thinking of how to develop the skills to move forward to their next belt. The belt is a way to show others your degree of commitment to your goals. The same can occur with respect to the degree with people in A.A. that want to demonstrate, by their example, that they have self-control. Whether in A.A., the Martial Arts, or in life – self-control begins with the ability to change the thing you can and let go of the rest.

"The Serenity Prayer perfectly sums that up. God, grant me the serenity to accept the things I cannot change, the courage to change the things I can. And the wisdom to know the difference."

BY KARL PAUL REINHOLD NIEBUHR

The idea of the intensity of feeling is that as you grow in understanding yourself, you will learn how to change a feeling that is negatively intense into something very different. Let's look at the word Anger concerning degree or intensity. A person can be full of rage or could just be angry, or we can go in the opposite direction, which is less intense so that you could feel just bitter or vexed. As you can see, there are different intensities in which to express yourself and explore. It is critical in recovery from addictions to develop a degree of understanding within ourselves to develop the self-confidence needed to practice virtuousness. I'm not asking that we become saints, I'm just asking you to practice on a daily basis a vocabulary of reason.

CHAPTER TWO

AUTHENTICITY

"Honesty is the cornerstone of character. The honest man or woman seeks not merely to avoid criminal or illegal act, but to be scrupulously fair, upright, and fearless in both action and expression. Honesty pays dividends both in dollars and in peace of mind."

B.C. FORBES

What do we do not to betray ourselves? Can an alcoholic indeed be authentic?

BORROWED FROM WWW.GOODREADS.COM, "AUTHENTICITY—IS BEING TRUE TO A VISION AND PURPOSE. WE ARE AUTHENTIC WHEN WE CHOOSE TO ACT AND FEEL AND CHOOSE TO BEHAVE IN BALANCE WITH THE HIGHER VALUES AND PRINCIPLES WE'VE CHOSEN FOR OUR LIVES…" BY BILL PITTMAN

Being authentic suggests that to live in truth, we have to ask ourselves, "Do I understand the Seven Deadly Sins, and can I live **my life** by the Seven Virtues?" What is essential here is to ask **ourselves** if we are **capable** of using **these** words of a moral nature, which are the opposite of the deadly sins? I always ask myself, "Am I ready to do the work, to practice integrating a list of words, which will follow in this book, and use these words to change my attitudes?"

Practicing martial arts gave me the self-discipline I needed to change. Being around people that have practiced the steps of A.A. or any other self-help system has helped me to acquire and develop the same self-discipline. There are great rewards in change. One phrase I use often is "to be impeccable with your word," which means to keep your word to yourself. We humans have an extraordinary brain. Even when we have spent some time messing it up, it has the ability to heal itself, provided we give it the information and fuel it needs to improve. We live with instincts and intellectual skills.

We must dig deep inside ourselves and learn our true nature. As an artist or a person on a quest to grow, I learned to practice the thoughts that come from asking myself questions surrounding words like, beliefs, values, and virtues. The primary purpose of this book is for you to question yourself. Ask a question, and your brain is pre-designed to seek an answer. What a gift God gave us all!

The bottom line is to understand that having rational thoughts and goals IS THE GOAL. We need to realize that in this day and age, the idea that emotions are the same as feelings is not the truth. They are different words, and they will be explained later in the book.

My academy, through my community of Black Belts and Masters throughout the world, proudly belongs to the Brotherhood of Martial Artists. The following is a brief synopsis of my BOMA patch.

The fingers of the left palm represent the four nurturing elements: **Virtue, Wisdom, Health,** and **Excellence**, which encompass the universal spirit of martial arts. The left thumb is slightly bent to imply one should never be arrogant or self-centered.

Conversely, the right-hand stands for rigorous practice and is clenched in a fist to symbolize attack, while the left, being righteous and disciplined, serves to restrain it, creating balance.

The Yin Yang image in the background further suggests that these forces are not opposing, but rather complementary, and form a dynamic system where the whole is greater than the sum of its parts. Similarly, practitioners from different disciplines form lasting alliances with one another, leading to a synergistic brotherhood of martial artists that span the globe.

The same premise applies to people that practice the ideas set in the twelve steps of Alcoholics Anonymous. Often you will hear people say, "His family, or his brothers and sisters, my name is, _____, and I'm an alcoholic." Often you will also hear, "I'm an addict or a user. I'm powerless, etc." The idea here is that those that practice due diligence, develop a sense of understanding needed to live with discipline and have the courage to adjust or tweak what is needed as they grow in sobriety and maturity.

The founder of modern-day Judo named Jigoro Kano wrote:

"MAXIMUM EFFICIENCY, MINIMAL EFFORT FOR THE MUTUAL WELFARE AND BENEFIT OF ALL." THERE'S A LESSON IN THAT.

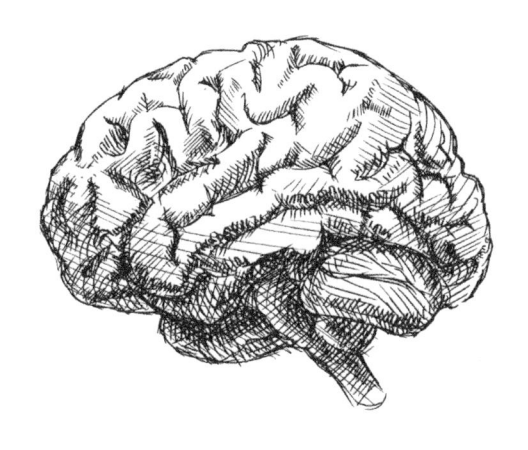

CHAPTER THREE

THE IDEOLOGY OF EMOTIONAL INTELLIGENCE

"Courage and perseverance have a magical talisman, before which difficulties disappear, and obstacles vanish into air."

JOHN QUINCY ADAMS

*The intellect has little to do on the road to discovery.
There comes a leap in consciousness, call it intuition
or what you will, and the solution comes to you,
and you don't know how or why. All great
discoveries are made in this way.*

ALBERT EINSTEIN

*"Anybody can become angry-that is easy; but to be angry
with the right person, and to the right degree, and at the right
time, and for the right purpose, and in the right way- that is
not within everybody's power and is not easy."*

ARISTOTLE

I reference the noble words of John Quincy Adam, Albert Einstein, and Aristotle for us to recognize the importance of deep thinking.

EMOTIONAL INTELLIGENCE

A critical key to success in sobriety is to acquire emotional literacy. Developing a working understanding of our list of *Feeling Words and Affirmations that Heal* is key to our growth and brings us in line with living the principle and promise of Step Seven. We need to understand where we fall short. Steps four, five, and six bring us to that understanding and prepare us to have God remove our shortcomings. My responsibility and actions are to practice developing Emotional Literacy. To do this, I must push myself past my comfort zones to behave with maturity in mind.

WHEN WE DO OUR BEST TO LIVE WITH MORALS, VIRTUES, AND RESPECT FOR OURSELVES AND OTHERS, WE BECOME CO-CREATORS. WE LISTEN TO GOD THROUGH MEDITATION BECAUSE IT IS THROUGH MEDITATION THAT WE FIGURE OUT HOW WE ARE SUPPOSED TO LIVE. GOD GAVE US EVERYTHING WE NEED AT BIRTH TO BE CO-CREATORS.

"Our ability to feel, name, and communicate our feelings is central to developing emotional literacy. When we can talk about what we're experiencing on a feeling level, we can use our thinking minds to make sense of our feelings' mind. We can use our reasoning to play a role in regulating and lending perspective on our emotional reactions."

TIAN DAYTON

EMOTIONAL SERENITY

The idea of emotional sobriety is closely linked to serenity, an unshakable sense of inner peace that people can find in recovery. The idea here is that we practice healthy re-scripting. Such as when you are feeling hateful, we turn it into understanding, or when we are feeling scared, we convert it into a sense of serenity. The idea again is to change unhealthy thinking or feelings into nurturing moments. It is the art of practicing nurturing words within our thoughts until it becomes a part of our psyche. This statement reflects on the idea of meditation. Meditation is a mindful moment of sincere reflection about any purpose which a person reveals on to change the things they can in themselves, again, known as re-scripting.

We say *The Serenity Prayer* at the end of meetings, which reminds us to use courage, right? It's a solemn reminder that it takes courage to take the time needed to think hard about what we want to change in ourselves and challenge ourselves to determine what our thoughts about emotional sobriety should be.

ARE EMOTIONS THE SAME AS FEELINGS?

Research shows that emotions and feelings are different. Our instincts are the emotions, the physical experiences we have when something happens, and we react to the situation in fractions of a second.

What we feel is the energy that comes from our Limbic system, just under the cerebral cortex in the brain. A couple of ways to think about this is to understand that the Limbic controls our basic emotions. These emotions are hard-wired in our bodies. We react to a variety of situations by instinct. These instincts are known as the fight or flight response people act out of when we are aware of something dangerous or surprised.

> TIAN DAYTON STATES, "WE ARE MEANT TO EXPERIENCE OUR BASIC EMOTIONS IN A SPLIT SECOND BEFORE WE HAVE TIME TO FEEL OUR FEELINGS SURROUNDING THEM. THAT CRUCIAL ONE-TENTH OF A SECOND MAY MEAN THE DIFFERENCE BETWEEN HEALTH AND INJURY."

Have you ever wondered why nature put first things first, safety above understanding? When we're startled, the thinking part of us temporarily shuts down for some very profound reasons. We aren't supposed to be distracted by any unnecessary thoughts when danger threatens. The hormone adrenaline floods our body, which enables us to either fight, flee, or freeze. To be still and remain unnoticed, to become invisible. This ancient fear instinct happens before any conscious thought enters our mind. The autonomic response system enables people to survive in dangerous situations. Our emotions naturally allow us to fight, flee, or freeze."

WHY FROZENNESS?

Counseling, A.A., and various support groups are designed to help people move from being frozen to being open. As the frozenness of those inner conflicts wears off in the safety of a therapeutic environment, we can then process the feelings that never really were processed during our formative stages in life. As an adult, we can mature within the safety and support of a healing environment. This process allows us to self-reflect, to witness situations from the past through our adult eyes of today. The last sentence warrants repeating, "This process allows us to self-reflect, to witness situations from the past through our adult eyes of today."

Much of the energy expended on emotions is on fear and anger. I hope we can focus on the fact that many people lose their ability to experience sound sobriety due to their inability to develop curiosity and composure, which are the opposites of fear and anger. As adults in A.A., we start to experience the attention we needed as children. As we develop, using Healing Words, (affirmations surrounding wellness), it becomes clear how to integrate our adult experience of today into healing our past youthful selves into a sense of personal groundedness.

WHAT IS EMOTIONAL SOBRIETY?

As the years have gone by, it has become evident to me that when thinking of the phrase, "half measures avail us nothing," could mean that once we obtain a year of clean and sober living, we will reach a point where we realize we need some emotional fine-tuning. When it comes to change, we also need to develop a more mature vocabulary in which to express ourselves, which can take place in three to five years. Then, all you must do is to continue to practice what you've changed in yourself. That's great news! That brings us to the letter from Bill W. written in 1958 called Emotional Sobriety, the Next Frontier.

What is emotional sobriety? Well, the quick answer is that emotional sobriety is the soundness of mind. It is the ability to experience your feelings at the moment. I believe that emotional sobriety is not so much about how we handle feeling good or bad, but how we perceive feeling good or bad, own the moment, and understand that we think the way we think because of our belief system and those things we value.

THE NEXT QUESTION TO ASK YOURSELF IS, "WHAT CAN I DO TO CHANGE MY OLD BELIEF SYSTEM INTO A NEW ADULT VERSION OF MYSELF?"

Growth occurs with the help of a counselor with whom you can become grounded and feel safe. Being restored to sanity isn't about not thinking you're not crazy anymore; it is about taking baby steps to learn how to re-script yourself with the help of a counselor. Then you have developed a healthy relationship that can help you develop the life skills of living in the moment, regardless of what that may be.

"Sometimes emotional sobriety is about tolerating what you are feeling. It is about staying sober no matter what you are feeling. It means that you don't have to blame yourself or your program because life can be challenging. It means that you don't necessarily need to do something to make the feeling go away."

PSYCHOLOGY TODAY MAGAZINE

One of the most helpful things we can do is develop the patience for our feelings to minimize. Let's face it, when we are startled, we experience a more intense feeling, but all feelings eventually reduce in intensity.

WE DECIDE WHAT WE FEEL

Emotions arise unconsciously throughout the day, and we mistakenly think they operate outside our control. Think of the following phrases and decide which thoughts blame others for the way you feel;

- She made me angry.
- I was overcome by fear.
- I was full of grief.
- I am overcome with remorse.

Those of us, who have ever suspended conscious control while under the influence of chemicals, stress, or obsessions, may tend to view feelings as totally independent entities. The truth is we select our feelings.

No matter how spontaneous feelings may seem, they are the result of complex internal processing of attitudes, memories, and expectations. I've learned to attach new scripts or views to old memories to place reasonable expectations on myself and others. I changed many attitudes because I have matured as a result of becoming grounded in my understanding of how to relate my feelings to life situations. Repeat, this is an important phrase. It's worth saying again with a slight twist. "How do I describe my feelings to situations that are outside my control?"

I know old memories are repairable, and because I don't want to give problems control over my emotions anymore, I continuously practice the new scripts daily until they become internalized.

The problem with attitudes, memories, and expectations is that they can be faulty. Alcoholic homes, with their insecurity and intolerance for expression of feelings, have taught many of us the **Don't Talk, Don't Trust, and Don't Feel Rules.**

Hence, we subsequently betrayed ourselves from receiving proper attention from those that are close to us. The continuing desire for some power (as well as love and acceptance) resulted in a fixation on shame, pain, and guilt.

By looking at our family patterns, we can see how we formed our attitudes. We then can make decisions about healing the past and changing our hopelessness and negative perceptions into hopefulness and growth toward potential.

WHEN I WAS YOUNG

When I was young, I experienced moments where I could look inside myself and feel the excitement of living the moment. I didn't have the burden of having to analyze what it was I was experiencing. Think about this for a minute -- remember what it was like when you went to the zoo and you were filled with the excitement of seeing all the animals?

Let's use those zoo animals, such as **Dolphins, Butterflies, Dogs, Gorillas,** and **Tigers,** to illustrate feelings. They were some of my favorites! I also genuinely enjoyed the majesty and the wonder of Dragons. In the following chapter, I will share with you all about these Big Six. I hope you enjoy it.

Thinking back in time when I was young gives me a chance to remember when I enjoyed the world of wonder. For example, think of a child first seeing a gorilla, and watching it demonstrate the physicality of its nature or pounding his chest when he was mad.

The joy that can come from this book is it can help create moments where we think openly about our past in the comfort of being open-minded. Which being open-minded is something we can do as adults.

All I'm doing here is directly suggesting mystical ideas, emotions, and states of mind. When I was growing up, my father used to tell me, "A picture speaks a thousand words." So, as you look at the pictures of all the animals in this book, my wish is that you experience your youth with a new point of view.

UNDERLYING FEELINGS

Begin by deciding what you want to experience and then evaluate the steps necessary to achieve those things. Every day that we are clean and sober, we have the opportunity to practice developing and nurturing ourselves to develop a stronger sense of self. The truth is there are so many different ways in which we choose how we're going to feel about day to day situations. The acceptance saying in the **Big Book** talks about when you are disturbed, it is because you find some person, place, thing, or situation unacceptable. So, again, the question necessary to ask is, "What needs to be adjusted in my belief system?" Each one of our beliefs is unique. And totally our own. So, am I adult enough today to practice using new ideas and values to become a better version of myself? Are you?

Many health and well-being professionals challenge each other on what the actual core feeling list should be and how it associates with the States of Being. Individuals in recovery who have a desire to reach a higher level of maturity will be willing to integrate these feelings into their daily life. If you find yourself having difficulty connecting with these feelings, then now is the time to push yourself past your comfort zone. Then you will experience the maturity that comes with practicing daily words, which by their very nature, will enhance your ability to verbalize your feelings and better understand the new sense of groundedness in your attitude to life. There will only be a few associated States of Being words attached to each Core Feeling. If this troubles the reader, please practice studying the list until it feels and becomes natural.

So, let us take a look at six underlying feelings. The challenge here is to adjust our old thinking and rethink the "Don't Talk, Don't Trust, and Don't Feel rules" we learned when we were young. During the ages of five through twelve, we learned underlying feelings and how to handle them through varying degrees.

As an adult, one of the neatest things we can do for ourselves is to rethink what is essential to how we feel about ourselves and others. We don't always have to agree with each other and feel precisely the same about how we view life challenges.

> **ONE AFFIRMATION I USE AND HELPS ME CONSIDERABLY IS, "I AGREE TO DISAGREE WITH YOUR POINT OF VIEW AND TO MY BEST ABILITY WILL *LIVE AND LET LIVE*."**

As an example, the feelings in this book are a fundamental guideline that you can use to practice and develop a strong sense of self. Here is what we say or think to ourselves to create or and change thought from Anger to Peace.

There is only one sentence we tell ourselves, which is, "When I feel _____; at this moment, I choose to own my feeling and change it to something healthier."

Many professionals will talk about a range of feelings; however, I speak in terms of degree because of my experience with the Martial arts. Examples of degrees might be Justifiable Anger, to Annoyance Anger, to Aggressive Anger, the good old-fashioned Temper Tantrum. The pages that follow explain a reasonable point of view about looking at our thoughts about feelings.

WHAT FOLLOWS ARE THE BIG SIX, WHICH ARE:

JOYFUL

Sad

MAD

Powerful

PEACEFUL

SCARED

CHAPTER FOUR

THE BIG SIX

After practicing martial arts for a few years, it became clear to me that my teacher was a wise man. Sometimes I wonder if it was wisdom or just being practical. Anyway, I discovered that I had many questions I needed to ask my teacher. Usually, our teacher is the go-to person for any questions we may have about our training at the dojang.

HERE'S AN EXAMPLE OF HOW A CONVERSATION MIGHT GO:

Student: *Master!*

Master: *Yes, Jeja.* (student)

Student: *I have a question about my feelings of anger.*

Master: *OK, how can I help?*

Student: *Well, sir, When I'm free fighting with someone on the mat, I feel I'm doing the right thing by being considerate to them, but I feel they take advantage of me being kind to them. I do my best to control myself. You always tell us that self-control is the goal of the martial artist. That self-control is a primary key in our ability to develop humility.*

Master: *I understand. So many people go around life acting like the Dragon. It seems like they only can behave like the Dragon and don't even realize that they are misbehaving. Please understand they walk around strutting their stuff and sticking their chest out to show off that they are tough, and that's because no one has challenged them to change. You will learn how to help them improve.*

Student: *How, Sir?*

Master: *You will teach them by example. You'll demonstrate good behavior. Right?*

Student: *Yes, Sir. I will do my best to change the things I can in myself. Sir, you know that I am in a recovery program - right?*

Master: *Yes!*

Student: *Sir, there's a saying I have learned, and it goes like this, "God grant me the serenity to accept the things I cannot change, courage to change the things I can, and the wisdom to know the difference."*

Master: *We have a saying in Korea called Jung Do, which is, "Right Thinking, Right Seeing, Right Listening, and Right Talking." So, it seems you are on the right path.*

Many times, I talked with my teacher about my feelings. I must say that his response would always bring about balance. Such as one man's sadness is another man's disappointment, or one man's anger is another man's courage.

LET'S GET TO IT.

The idea is to read through this book and discover in yourself those areas that you know you need to fine-tune. You will be a happier person for taking the time.

The following is a list of **what I call the big six commonly expressed feelings** used by individuals in self-help programs. To learn how to discriminate between feeling powerful or sad is how we learn to practice distinguishing between happy or sad or mad and glad. These six feelings which follow will help you reconnect yourself with being able to express yourself some of the most commonly expressed opinions and thoughts concerning these feeling in their varying degrees.

The ability to experience a variety of feelings is our goal. It is the same thing as training for your green belt after you have achieved your yellow belt in the arts. We set goals for ourselves and then achieve them.

JOYFUL

JOYFUL AS A DOLPHIN AND THEIR AMAZING CREATIVITY.

The dolphin often represents creativity, which is a tenet used in Martial Arts. We explain to students that using the word creativity invokes creative visualization and activates our "mind's eye" – that's the part of the mind that manages creativity. It also helps to give us the ability to practice meditation.

The dolphin can also represent a feeling of being joyful and having peace of mind. Creativity sparks other words such as contentment, calmness, or even a carefree mindset. Adopting a spirit of joyfulness allows us to skip rope with our kids, have a balloon fight in the back yard, and lean into the spirit of play. When we are carefree, we tend to have an open mind and a stronger ability to **Live and Let Live.**

SAD

2

SAD AS THE PUG DOG BUT OPTIMISTIC.

When you look at this little pug, you can't help to think about there is only one way to go, and that is up. This is why I say that the Dog represents being optimistic, which is another tenet that is practiced in the Martial Arts. I explain to students that using the word confident is similar to what is called being positive. We don't always feel optimistic, but we do know that we are capable of it. Ever notice how most dogs just want love, attention, and friendship? (Man's best friend and all!) Many are friendly simply because that is how they are by nature.

When we experience sadness or a deep sense of grief, it would be beneficial to remember that you can change that feeling—a synonym such as feeling empty rather than sad. I can feel a little upset rather than anxious. When I am usually sad, I typically feel misunderstood.

It is critical to surround yourself with people that have sound sobriety because they have most likely practiced the ability to stay grounded, keep sadness and sorrow at bay, and live in gratitude

MAD

3

MAD AS A GORILLA BUT TENACIOUS AND DETERMINED.

For many, Gorillas represent being tenacious and determined. Tenacious is another tenet that Martial Artists use to overcome the feeling of weakness rather than to get angry about things over which we have no control. We explain to students that using the word Tenacity or the phrase "indomitable spirit" is similar to what is called being stern. Ever notice how a Gorilla is always trying to guard his territory? People in recovery are continually striving to protect their EGO. The seventh step teaches us how to go about our business politely and with modesty.

The ability to experience a variety of feelings is our goal. It is the same thing as training for your green belt after you have achieved your yellow belt in the arts. We set goals for ourselves and then execute them. It seems that the feeling of being mad gives people a false sense of strength. That's why I use the idea of a Gorilla. Imagine the power and determination of a gorilla to protect himself from a perceived enemy. I must say that alcoholics are very defensive, just like the gorilla. We do get mad as hell, but we fail to have the ability to express ourselves as well a gorilla.

POWERFUL

4

THE DRAGON IS A POWERFUL MYSTIC CREATURE AND DEMONSTRATES INDOMITABLE SPIRIT.

Dragons are known for their air of mystery. People in recovery act like the Dragon due to their guarded behavior. Addicts are concerned with what they have done in the past and don't want to be held accountable for any of it. However, once we get honest with ourselves, we are willing to make amends for our wrongdoings. People in recovery are continually striving to protect their EGO. In Martial arts, the Dragon represents heaven. I can't help but think that step three is the starting point for thinking of heaven.

We can experience a feeling of power and a sense of might when we think about the nature of the Dragon, which can lead to fascinating thoughts and questions. How can I expand my view of life? How can I increase my sense of confidence and calm? Now imagine you have a dragon as a pet, and it is walking around with you everywhere. How confident would you be then? Channel your inner Dragon!

PEACEFUL

5

THE GRACEFULNESS AND PEACEFULNESS OF THE BUTTERFLY, REPRESENTING HARMONY AND BALANCE.

A Butterfly represents harmony, which is a tenet that Martial Artists use to overcome the feeling of fear. We explain to students that using the word balance is similar to desiring humility. Ever notice how the thought of a butterfly is calming and peaceful?

People in recovery would benefit significantly if they thought about the Butterfly and its grace. Another synonym to harmony might be serenity. Something we all strive to have.

SCARED

6

THE TIGER IS A SCARY BUT COURAGEOUS CAT.

    A tiger can represent Courage. Being courageous is a tenet that Martial Artists use to overcome the feeling of self-doubt. As martial artists, we learn to challenge ourselves, which I integrated into my A.A. experiences. Rather than get caught up in what others try to make us believe and create awkward situations, we explain to students that using the word courage is similar to being brave. Being strong builds self-confidence. You can only experience confidence; it cannot be taught. Ever notice how the thought of a tiger can be scary or maybe to some exciting? People in recovery would benefit if they acted with the bravery of a tiger. The Tiger can be mysterious and a cunning predator. Martial artists, like the Tiger, hide in waiting to surprise the opponent. Karate practitioners develop explosive techniques. Humans have primal instincts that we sometimes forget. The emotions we experience in a fraction of a second when startled or in danger call on us to be courageous. Feelings are the rational response to that fraction of a second occurrence.

I had an experience with a student's mother who took pride in what we talk about in class and how it affects her daughter and moves other parents. She respects what I say in class, and the many conversations we have had over the years. We talked about what she wrote concerning one of the principles I have on my website, under the heading of Mission, the Character Concept Corner. These lists of traits that are important to me as a teacher, and I believe it should be relevant to my students. Ultimately, I think that many of the words in my Character Concept Corner can help people tremendously in recovery; and those who face a multitude of other addictions that haunt people.

Everything I have tried to do since starting the martial arts, going to school, and working with alcoholics is to integrate the tools and mindsets that I was not given in my younger years. I now teach individuals of all walks of life the deep values that come from having developed emotional sobriety and soundness of mind. To focus on change is difficult, but to focus on not changing is infinitely more difficult. We can personally grow by leaps and bounds by choosing to practice the thought or affirmation that says, "I can get a lot done a little bit at a time."

I WANT TO SHARE SOMETHING A GOOD FRIEND WROTE WITH ME IN MIND FOR YOU. SHE WISHES TO REMAIN ANONYMOUS BECAUSE SHE IS PRACTICING SOMETHING THAT SHE LEARNED FROM ME, WHICH IS, "WHAT DOES IT TAKE TO BE A SILENT CHAMPION?"

Tenet is just one of twenty-four attributes expressed by my dear friend. As you read forward, there are those words or statements that I think will jump out at you, such as:

- Independent action
- High achievement
- Harness the power of curiosity
- Demonstrate initiative and the rewards of self-directed behavior

WHY DOES GRANDMASTER HUTSON EMPHASIZE THE CHARACTER TRAIT OF INITIATIVE?

FOSTERING SELF-DIRECTED BEHAVIOR

Great students come in all shapes and sizes. Whether observing classes in the academic world or out on the mat, what sets them apart is not their mental abilities, or even their physical skills, but rather their inner drive.

Independent action is the key to success. Individuals who regularly take charge of their training, and consistently put forth their best efforts, attain excellence. Top students understand the importance of repetition and review their studies willingly. For them, outside recognition is often downplayed because they compete with themselves. High achievers know how to harness the power of curiosity to fight boredom by delving into subjects deeper. Ordinary life transforms into an exciting adventure.

By contrast, in today's culture, it is not uncommon for people to do only what is necessary to get by—at school and on the job. But so much potential is lost with this limiting perspective. How does one demonstrate initiative and reap the rewards of self-directed behavior?

Be proactive about the learning process. Practice on your own without being told to do so. Focus on the journey, not just the result. Don't look to others for motivation but show your commitment and challenge yourself to become better than you were yesterday. As we continue to grow in the spirit of emotional sobriety, it is necessary to understand the word proactive also to mean having the ability to take the initiative.

CHAPTER FIVE

THE FIX FOR DEFECTS OF CHARACTER

"To have a respect for ourselves guides our morals, and to have deference for others governs our manners."

LAURENCE STERNE

So, here we go again, looking at the fix for those horrible defects of character. If you are asking yourself what the fix is, I can tell you the most straightforward answer there is: **living a life of virtue and humility.** The virtues I'm referring to which are the opposite of the character defects are:

HUMILITY

KINDNESS

Charity

PURITY

Composure

SELF-RESTRAINT

DILIGENCE

Ask yourself, "How can I develop the ability to understand all that I needed to learn when I was a teenager, but didn't?" That's a big question. What do you need to learn – and most importantly, unlearn – to live a life of virtue and humility?

We were all gifted with free will – but sometimes that gets the best of us, doesn't it? All those choices, between the right thing and the wrong thing. The easy thing and putting in the work for the not so easy stuff.

According to the twelve and twelve (Twelve Steps and Twelve Traditions), there is a universally recognized list of human failings called the Seven Deadly Sins. They are:

PRIDE

ENVY

GLUTTONY

LUST

GREED

SLOTH

ANGER

THE BOTTOM LINE?

We are supposed to focus on the universally recognized failings, so we can develop into being reasonable and responsible human beings.

DEADLY SINS ... VIRTUE

PRIDE - *Vanity* ... Humility

ENVY - *Jealousy* ... Kindness

GREED - *Avarice* ... Charity-Giving

LUST - *Sexual Appetites* ... Chastity-Purity

ANGER - *Hate* ... Forgiveness-Composure

GLUTTONY - *Indulgence* ... Self-Restraint

SLOTH - *Laziness* ... Diligence-Labor

In the following pages are the American Heritage Dictionary meanings of the Deadly Sins along with their synonyms. Following each Defect of Character (Deadly Sin), there are Virtues necessary to change and grow. From these, we can learn to see where we stand within ourselves so we can challenge ourselves to grow beyond our current understanding. Step Seven allows us to take a serious look at where we need to improve our character and actions.

As you'll notice throughout the next chapter, there are pictures of animals that are attached to each feeling word and Defect of Character. My wish for you is to understand your instincts and how they connect us, mentally, emotionally, and instinctually to the animal kingdom.

CHAPTER SIX

SEVEN DEADLY SINS & CORRESPONDING VIRTUES

"Good character is that quality which makes one dependable whether being watched or not, which makes one truthful when it is to one's advantage to be a little less than truthful, which makes one courageous when faced with great obstacles, which endows one with the firmness of wise self-discipline."

ARTHUR S. ADAMS

The main reason this chapter will focus on the seven deadly sins is that the twelve and twelve (Twelve Steps and Twelve Traditions) talks about not falling into confusion over the names of the defects of character that alcoholics have and making a connection that alcoholics share the very nature of humanity's shortcomings described in the **Big Book of Alcoholics Anonymous:** our shortcomings.

As we continue to read about the seven deadly sins, we must understand that the whole point of reviewing them is to look at the opposite of each; and to look at ourselves as rational human beings. By doing so, this will help us develop a more balanced sense of our feelings and better able to connect to other people. The character defects talked about in the **Big Book of Alcoholics Anonymous**, can be challenged and understood by using virtue as the principle, which hopefully will help us change the things we can in ourselves.

SO, LET US TAKE A LOOK AT HOW WE CAN RE-SCRIPT OUR LIVES WITH VIRTUES RATHER THAN DEFECTS.

PRIDE

PRIDE OF THE PEACOCK

Peacocks are a large pheasant known for their beautiful colored feathers. Their tail feathers, also called coverts, make up more than 60 percent of the bird's total body length, with only males having the colorful blue and iridescent green feathers.

So, when you think about it, the Peacock struts and strides with a sense of cockiness.

PRIDE VERSUS HUMILITY

The Defect of Character **"Pride"** is a sense of one's own proper dignity or value, self-respect, and an unreasonable sense of pleasure or satisfaction taken in an achievement, arrogance, or disdainful conduct or treatment. Usually, the word pride denotes an excessive nature.

The following is a list of some common synonyms, which I hope will help in understanding other points of view when reflecting on and understanding pride within ourselves.

There is a lot to be said about pride and the many synonyms which follow that help to give you other insights into the nature of pride.

EGO

VANITY

Conceit

Narcissism

SUPERIORITY

Arrogance

PRESUMPTION

The Virtue of Pride is **"Humility,"** being the quality or condition of being humble. Here is a list of some commonly used synonyms for humility.

HUMILITY

MEEKNESS

MODESTY

Attitude

JOYFUL SPIRIT

Composure

NOT ARROGANT

Deferential

SUBMISSIVE

You can utilize the process in this book to change old ideas, hence, allowing you to reflect on creating new ideas, and values in your life. Begin to develop your list of words, and you will gradually develop new attitudes. The words you accept into your psyche will, in turn, help you create a certain degree of happiness inside yourself.

ENVY

ENVY OF THE PANDA

Pandas live mainly in forests high in the mountains of western China, where they subsist almost entirely on bamboo. They must eat from 26 to 84 pounds of bamboo every day, a formidable task for which they use their enlarged wrist bones that function as opposable thumbs. Most would say that Panda has a simple life. Who wouldn't want to have that?

ENVY VERSUS KINDNESS

The Defect of Character **"Envy"** is a feeling of discontent and resentment aroused by and in conjunction with desire for the possessions or qualities of another.

Here is a list of some commonly used synonyms, which I hope will help you to be better able to change your thoughts and feelings about it and change your vocabulary to reflect the virtue rather than the vice.

Some examples of synonyms for envy would be:

JEALOUSY

Covetousness

Enviousness

COVET

KINDNESS

The Virtue to Envy is **"Kindness"** seen as the quality or state of being kind, an instance of altruistic behavior. Here is a list of some commonly used synonyms for kindness:

CHARITABLENESS

SERVICE TO OTHERS

Favor benevolence

Grace

INDULGENCE

Charity

Re-scripting envy into kindness is rewarding and healthy. Write the list from above onto a small piece of paper and carry it around with you so you can look at them ever so often. This is one way to practice little changes.

GREED

THE GREED OF THE FOX

Fox-like features typically include a triangular face, pointed ears, an elongated rostrum, and a bushy tail. Foxes are digitigrades, and thus, walk on their toes. Unlike most members of the family canines, foxes have partially retractable claws. The fable of the fox is that they are excessive about what they need.

GREED VERSUS CHARITY

The Defect of Character **"Greed"** is an excessive desire to acquire or possess more than what one needs or deserves, especially concerning material wealth. Here is a list of some common synonyms for greed:

AVARICE

Covetousness

Acquisitiveness

AVIDITY

CHARITY

The Virtue of Greed is **"Charity,"** is a provision of help or relief to the poor. The idea of the virtue of charity can be demonstrated by giving to help the needy, alms, a relief institution or organization, or a fund established to help others or humanity. Here is a list of some commonly used synonyms:

TOLERANCE

INDULGENCE

Charitableness

Forbearance

LENIENCY

Kind

Compassion

Use these kind words to help challenge your old thought and belief patterns regarding greed. Write the list from above onto a small piece of paper and carry it around with you so you can look at them ever so often. This is one way to practice little changes. Re-scripting greed into charity is rewarding and healthy.

LUST

LUST OF THE RABBIT

Rabbits are meticulously clean animals and are easy to housebreak and train. Happy rabbits practice acute behavior known as a "binky:" This is when they jump up in the air and twist and spin around! A baby rabbit is called a kit, a female is called a doe, and a male is a buck. A group of rabbits is called a herd. Usually, by association, people that have many kids are referred to like people that have sex like rabbits. Why? Their gestation period is just 31 days, and they produce six to eight babies in a litter!

LUST VERSUS CHASTITY

The Defect of Character **"Lust,"** is an intense or unrestrained sexual craving: an overwhelming desire or need. Here is a list of some common synonyms to re-script:

DESIRE

HUNGER

Yearning

Longing

CRAVING

Sexual hunger

PASSION

CHASTITY

The Virtue of Lust is **"Chastity,"** it is the condition or quality of being pure or chaste. Here is a list of some commonly used synonyms, virtuous character,

CELIBACY

PURITY

Decency

Modesty

VIRTUOUSNESS

Use these words to begin to change the way you look and perceive lust. Write the list from above onto a small piece of paper and carry it around with you so you can look at them ever so often. This is one way to practice little changes. Re-scripting lust into chastity is rewarding and healthy.

ANGER

THE ANGER OF THE ELEPHANT

Elephants are famous for their incredible memories and their superior intelligence. They are notorious for their violent rage and sometimes fatal outbursts. Their strength and affinity for excitement make elephants one of the most potentially dangerous animals in the world. A rocking motion often precedes the elephant's excited behavior. Both wild and captive elephants can be violent in stressful situations, but this is more common in those kept in a zoo or circus.

ANGER VERSUS FORGIVENESS

The Defect of Character **"Anger"** is a strong feeling of displeasure or hostility. Here is a list of some common synonyms for anger:

RAGE

FURY

Wrath

Resentment

INDIGNATION

Violence

They represent degrees of feeling. These nouns denote varying degrees of marked displeasure anger, the most general, is strong displeasure. Indignation is righteous anger at something regarded as being wrongful, unjust, or evil.

FORGIVENESS

The Virtue of Anger is **"Forgiveness"** is the act of forgiveness or to pardon. Here is a list of some commonly used synonyms for forgiveness:

EXCUSE

PARDON

Condone

Remit

FORGIVE

Mercy

Use these words or ones that feel most comfortable for you to pivot from anger to forgiveness in your life. Write the list from above onto a small piece of paper and carry it around with you so you can look at them ever so often. This is one way to practice little changes. Re-scripting anger into forgiveness is rewarding and healthy.

GLUTTONY

GLUTTONY OF THE HOG

As children, we learned what made us feel happy. Television, Matchbox cars, Swimming pools. Bicycles. Candy. Chocolate. Ice cream and Chips. For many people, junk food triggers the release of dopamine, a happiness hormone, in the brain.

GLUTTONY VERSUS TEMPERANCE

The Defect of Character **"Gluttony,"** is excess in eating or drinking. Here is a list of some common synonyms that relate to gluttony:

OVEREATING

GORMANDIZING

Hoggishness

Immoderation

TEMPERANCE

The Virtue of Gluttony is **"Temperance,"** as in moderation, self-restraint, behavior, or expression. Restraint in the use of or abstinence from alcohol or other addictive substances. Here is a list of some commonly used synonyms:

MODERATION

MODERATENESS

Abstinence

Sobriety

SOBERNESS

Use these words to encourage you to stay focused on your sobriety. Write the list from above onto a small piece of paper and carry it around with you so you can look at them ever so often. This is one way to practice little changes. Re-scripting gluttony into temperance is rewarding and healthy.

SLOTH

LAZY AS THE SLOTH

Sloths represent laziness and indifference. It is common to identify lazy people with those innocent mammals, as well. Patience and meditation are the opposite sides of that coin. Sloths teach us the importance of patience. They are also associated with reflection, individual spiritual journey, introspection, and so on.

SLOTH VERSUS DILIGENCE

The Defect of Character "Sloth" is the aversion to work or exertion. Here is a list of some common synonyms for sloth-like behavior:

LAZINESS

IDLENESS

Loafing

Shiftlessness

SLOTHFULNESS

SLUGGISHNESS

DILIGENCE

The Virtue of Sloth is **"Diligence,"** the act of careful and persistent work or effort and the persistent application to an undertaking. Here is a list of some commonly used synonyms for diligence:

CONSCIENTIOUSNESS

ATTENTIVE CARE

Perseverance

Tenacity

Use these words to change your perspective from laziness to vigilant! Write the list from above onto a small piece of paper and carry it around with you so you can look at them ever so often. This is one way to practice little changes. Re-scripting sloth into diligence is rewarding and healthy.

CHAPTER SEVEN

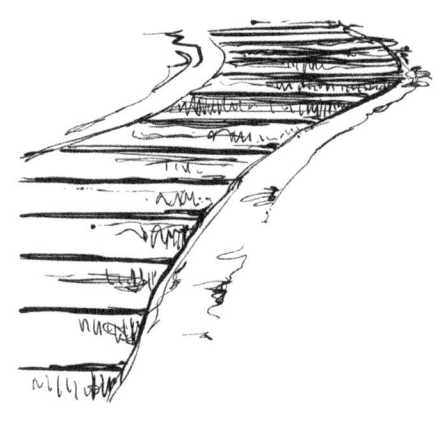

THE SEVENTH STEP

"Some persons are always ready to level those above them down to themselves, while they are never willing to level those below them up to their position. But he that is under the influence of true humility will avoid both these extremes. On the one hand, he will be willing that all should rise just so far as their diligence and worth of character entitle them to; and on the other hand, he will be willing that his superiors should be known and acknowledged in their place, and have rendered to them all the honors that are their due."

JONATHAN EDWARDS

The Seventh Step of Alcoholics Anonymous is to ask Him to humbly remove our shortcomings. Our desire for personal growth is critical in developing and educating ourselves. Utilizing a list of words, healing in nature, is a healthy way in which to advance our literacy and self-confidence. The willingness to develop a list of words to create a vocabulary that can identify our feelings so that we can live with ourselves is critical to maintaining stable sobriety. In turn, it helps to develop the art of self-discovery and maturity, which becomes an extraordinary new way to think for those in recovery. As we make progress in our recovery, we realize the real value of step seven. We recognize how important the idea of being virtuous is on our new journey of sobriety.

One of the critical discoveries in healing is in the realization that we are worthwhile individuals. We start to understand the value of not being overly prideful. Balance is the key. Remember that humility is the tool we use to become the best version of ourselves. The idea that we have to always look for someone or something outside of ourselves to feel whole is flawed. The truth is that God gave everyone everything we need to be a valued human being at birth.

HUMILITY IS A VIRTUE, A STATE OF BEING.

AS SUCH, THE DESIRE FOR HUMILITY MUST BE A DISCIPLINE TO BE DEVELOPED, JUST LIKE EVERY OTHER ATTITUDE. IN DEVELOPING HUMILITY, WE ARE FACED ONCE AGAIN WITH THE IDEA OF ACTIVE SURRENDER.

Asking God to remove our shortcomings, we must move and act in a manner that reflects our willingness to surrender. Remember, challenge your fear; it is essential to practice stepping out of our comfort zone. Fear is only unused energy.

In the words of Bill W..., "The chief activator of our defects has been self-centered fear--primarily fear that we would lose something we already possessed or would fail to get something we demanded."

You can find the just mentioned statement by Bill W. in the book **The Twelve Steps and Twelve Traditions.** At the end of the chapter on the seventh step, you will find this in the last two paragraphs.

CHAPTER EIGHT

TRANSFORMING OUR FEELINGS INTO WORDS

"Your living is determined not so much by what life brings to you as by the attitude you bring to life; not so much by what happens to you as, by the way, your mind looks at what happens. Circumstances and situations do color life, but you have been given the mind to choose what the color shall be."

JOHN HOMER MILLER

Emotional literacy is the ability to develop a vocabulary that will help you to translate your emotions and feelings into words that can be shared with another person. Sharing our experiences from one moment to another is a natural outgrowth of sound emotional development and maturity.

To attain and maintain emotional sobriety, we need to learn to tolerate our sometimes-conflicting feelings, which we know are childish and translate those feelings into reasonable words that can resonate within us. The ability to use our mind to organize our thoughts occurs through our limbic mind. Learning about the limbic system is an exciting new area to research and learn about what makes us tick and how our bodies function. It is a big key to developing and maintaining emotional maturity, balance, and sobriety.

Two phrases stand out amongst to me that can make a genuine difference in living with your word to yourself:

SELF-CONTROL AND SELF-DISCIPLINE.

"Our emotions are the driving powers of our lives. When we arouse emotionally, unless we do something great and good, we are in danger of letting our emotions become perverted. William James used to tell the story of a Russian woman who sat weeping at the tragic fate of the hero in the opera while her coachman froze to death outside."

- EARL RINEY

CHAPTER NINE

WORDS THAT HEAL

Before continuing, let's get clear about the word "heal." Although this is not a textbook definition, it serves as a clearer understanding of what is intended: "to become sound in opinion, to become physically healthy, and to make oneself whole." In exercising our courage to change the things we can, which is part of the serenity prayer, and with a focus on building on the work done in Steps Four and Five and five, now is an excellent time to educate yourself on words that have healing properties.

The following list of words is designed to strengthen your spirit and your mind. The effort to put our attention on healthy and healing thoughts is exercising our willingness, which is expressed in step six and to do our part in working on the areas in which we have fallen short. Meaning, in the seventh step, we recognize that our Higher Power wants us to develop and grow. Another way to say this is that God wants us to become the best possible version of ourselves.

LET'S TAKE A LOOK AT SOME WORDS IN ALPHABETICAL ORDER.

In my experience, whichever word jumps out at me first are the words I most likely need to practice integrating into my experience at that time to transform myself into my best possible self. Think of it as your intuition or conscience speaking to you to address the things you need to change in yourself.

The alphabet has 26 letters. Our goal is to take a word or two from each letter and practice integrating them into our daily lives. We are all capable of developing or re-scripting our vocabulary. There is no doubt in my mind that anybody that invests the same energy they put into using a drug and takes the initiative to practice change can apply the same energy into nurturing themselves into being a well-rounded individual who can achieve anything they set their minds to here is a good start.

A *Accepting, Agreeable, Appreciate, Approving, Aware*

B *Balance, Beautiful, Brilliant*

C *Carefree, Calm, Cheerful, Civil, Conscious*

D *Decisive, Determined, Devoted, Diplomatic*

E *Empathy, Energetic, Expressive, Ethical*

F *Fair, Flexible, Forgiving, Fun, Funny*

G *Generous, Gentle, Giving, Gracious, Grateful*

H *Helpful, Honest, Honoring, Humble, Humorous*

I *Inspire, Intuitive, Inventive, Inviting*

J *Joyful, Just, Jubilant*

K *Kind, Kindred, Kindhearted*

L *Loving, Loyal*

M *Merciful, Modest*

N *Nurturing, Nature*

O *Outgoing, Observant, Open, Optimistic*

P   *Patient, Peaceful, Playful, Polite, Principled*

Q   *Quarrelsome, Queasy, Quiet*

R   *Receptive, Reliable, Respectful, Responsible*

S   *Satisfied, Serene, Sensitive, Silly, Spontaneous,*

T   *Tender, Thoughtful, Tolerant, Trusting, Truthful*

U   *Unselfish, unbiased, unbalanced*

V   *Valiant, vanquished, vexed, vibrant, vulnerable*

W   *Warm, Wonderful, Whimsical*

X   *Xenial, Xenium*

Y   *Yearn, Yes, Yield, Youth*

Z   *Zany, Zeal, Zest*

When we were kids in kindergarten, we sang the nursery rhyme that went like this, "Now I know my A, B, C's tell me what you think of me." Now it's probably playing in your head, right? Words have real power. Pick your favorites or add new ones that resonate most with you to this list.

CHAPTER TEN

POWER PATTERNS IN HUMAN ATTITUDES

"The great composer does not set to work because he is inspired but becomes inspired because he is working. Beethoven, Wagner, Bach, and Mozart settled down day after day to the job in hand with as much regularity as an accountant settles down each day to his figures. They didn't waste time waiting for inspiration."

ERNEST NEWMAN

A.A. STANDS FOR ANONYMOUS AND ATTITUDE ADJUSTMENT. THE ABILITY TO BE WILLING TO LET GO OF YOUR OLD IDEAS AND INTEGRATE NEW IDEAS IS CRITICALLY IMPORTANT.

The ability to understand the difference between higher and lower energies is a fundamental process of maturity.

To grow in the spirit of Step Seven, I strongly encourage you to read the book *Power VS. Force* by David R. Hawkins M.D., Ph.D., and read over the list of words on pages 150 & 151 that Dr. Hawkins researched and has been proven to be extremely useful in changing our perceptions and behaviors. It is an immensely powerful read for those in recovery.

I strongly encourage counselors, life coaches, sponsors, and mentors to take the time to study this book as well. Notice I said to study the book, not just read it. It is complicated just to read a book one or two times and think that it will help achieve mental clarity. As a tool to clarify what I am referring to regarding these healthy words to integrate into your life, I am listing just a few examples from Doctor Hawkins's book. Please keep in mind that the list that is found in Dr. Hawkin's book adds up to one hundred and thirty-six contrasting pairs. So, here are just ten examples of what I am talking about, which is to see the positive and negative contrast.

POSITIVE ... NEGATIVE

Agreeable ... *Condescending*

Being ... *Having*

Choosing to ... *Having to*

Democratic ... *Dictatorial*

Empathetic ... *Pitying*

Flexible ... *Rigid*

Global ... *Local*

Healing ... *Irritating*

Inspired ... *Mundane*

Modest ... *Haughty*

Any person that gives serious thought to this shortlist, or better still, further investigating this list by studying Dr. Hawking's book will find that the list will help you become the best version of yourself. Practicing the healthy left side of this list and other lists of similar nature will ultimately help you create the shift to becoming a different person. The bottom line is that any person who dedicates a healthy or reasonable amount of time to these lists will grow in character and maturity.

Many of the words we speak are automatic reactions based on our belief system. Being aware of our words can reveal a great deal if you know what to look for – and what you should look for are healthy Power Patterns.

As mentioned earlier, the book *Power VS. Force* is a profound read and should prove a powerful resource when you are ready to do your seventh step on your journey to sobriety. For me, it was an exciting way to spark real and healthy change.

Power Patterns are words that tap into our positive energy and flow, creating a connection with your higher self. When we are more in tune with our higher self and practice choosing to stay in a healthy awareness of our feelings, we become connected to our spiritual source and thereby empowered to practice the seven virtues in our daily lives effectively. Those seven virtues are:

1. HUMILITY
2. KINDNESS
3. CHARITY
4. CHASTITY
5. FORGIVENESS
6. TEMPERANCE
7. DILIGENCE

These virtues are not something that improves overnight, but over time, can help us steer our lives more virtuously – and soberly.

CHAPTER ELEVEN

THE POWER OF AFFIRMATIONS

What you say is what you get. This simple statement demonstrates one of the most critical tools of spiritual self-development. Let us briefly explore the nature of affirmations and how you can use them to shape your inner reality.

An affirmation is a positive and healthy thought or idea that you consciously focus on to produce the desired result in yourself, such as a sense of calm and well-being. Affirmations help to smooth the process of shifting old ideas and mindsets to newer, healthier, happier alternatives. They can help heal you – and create a significant transformation in your life and move you in the direction of becoming the person you've always wanted to be.

HERE ARE A FEW EXAMPLES:

1. The highest reward of effort is not what I get from it, but who I become from it.
2. Life isn't about finding myself; it's about creating myself.
3. The more I trust my intuition; the more prosperity comes my way.
4. My intuition will show me the way.
5. My understanding of my past pain comes from my trying to shape my beliefs to others' expectations, which aren't mine.
6. By trusting my core values, I can change and adjust myself and become grounded in my truth. My desire to be authentic will lead me to truthfulness.
7. Delays give me time to prepare for the good that awaits me.
8. My world of nature embraces every cell of my being.
9. I am living a life of purpose and passion.
10. My greatest glory is in rising every time I fall.

After you have completed your steps through step five, re-scripting yourself is possible by practicing the affirmations that mean something to you. The daily practice helps facilitate growth and maturity. The statements are declarations for your independence.

For many, they are an essential tool for letting go of old habits, family beliefs or damaging belief systems, and becoming more grounded and healthier. Letting go of some of your parents' expectations and developing some of your own affirmations is critical. That's not disrespectful to your parents. It's merely developing the ability to become more respectful of yourself.

AFFIRMATIONS ARE POWERFUL GROUNDING TOOLS THAT, PRACTICED DAILY, EVEN SEVERAL TIMES PER DAY, CAN BECOME EXCELLENT TOOLS FOR MINDFULNESS, TRUTH, AND SOBRIETY.

CHAPTER TWELVE

CHARACTER TRAITS

When talking about character, we use the word traits to describe what your character is and is not. As you read forward, you may experience new points of view as we talk about the core traits of most individuals. What is neat about this is that you will discover that you may already have many of these qualities.

After doing your fourth step and are practicing your seventh step, I am sure that you will be able to recognize where you fall short of where you are experiencing some glaring behaviors you know you need to change but have had difficulty in doing so.

IT IS ESSENTIAL, AT THIS TIME, TO RECOGNIZE THAT YOU ARE ALSO LIVING WITH GOOD CHARACTER TRAITS RATHER THAN JUST FOCUSING ON YOUR SHORTCOMINGS. YOU ARE STRIVING FOR BALANCE.

LET'S LOOK AT THE VALUES THAT ARE GOOD AND BAD.

Those that you know you have been trying to change and those that you may not even have been aware of (both good and bad) up to this point. I've found many parallels between self-help and sobriety values and foundations with those practiced in the Martial Arts.

For me, these practices have been instrumental in my sobriety and in helping me to become the best version of myself. Two ideas that were introduced to me that stuck were the questions, "What does it take to be a gentleman?" and "What does it take to be a master?" The word gentleman introduces a standard of politeness, consideration, and appreciation towards oneself and others.

I connected the word master to the gentleman. Many people may think that a master is tough, as related to fighting. In some ways, the idea of being strict, for me, is less about exerting power and much more about strength, respect, and practicing the tenets of Martial Arts. Will you sometimes fall short? Absolutely! But the purpose of the seventh step in recovery is to help us recognize our shortcomings and be willing to practice wherever and whatever to correct those negative points of view.

The martial arts tenets include courtesy, which is the showing of politeness in one's attitude and behavior towards others. Integrity, perseverance, self-control, and indomitable spirit are other tenants practiced daily. My goal has been to merge the virtues/tenets of the Twelve Steps of A.A. into my practice and teaching of the Martial Arts and to mentor people in the fellowship of self-help to integrate the values of the martial arts into their daily lives.

LET'S FACE IT, TO DEVELOP SOBRIETY OR SOUNDNESS OF MIND TAKES A LOT OF PRACTICE.

Fundamentally that means that if you practice the twelve steps and integrate the ideas, teachings, and strategies of whatever fellowship you choose to be in, you will discover a new level of happiness and serenity

Let's talk about traits that are important to character development. Many of us didn't have parental help. Many looked at what it took to change and thought it too steep a hill to climb. Whatever your life experience, know that you can now use it to build a new adventure – one based on virtue, sobriety, and even happiness.

In the following pages, we will review character traits that are essential to achieving ***Emotional Sobriety.*** How do I know these traits are necessary? Because I never ask anyone to do anything that I haven't already done myself. If I haven't done it, and I'm asking you to do something, then I will do it right along with you. This way, I/We become aware of one particular way in which we learn, grow, and get to know ourselves:

SELF-KNOWLEDGE

SELF-AWARENESS

Self-Acceptance

Self-esteem

SELF-ACTUALIZATION

Before we can expect anything from other people, we must first apply the expectations that we have of others to ourselves.

When we are positive, the attitudes that help us experience the feeling of joyfulness are:

OPTIMISM

ACCEPTANCE

Cheerfulness

Enthusiasm

BEING A GOOD SPORT

Humility

GRATITUDE

The idea of having some kind of joy in our lives seems to be what so many individuals are trying to achieve. Hence, the one freedom I have is the ability to practice new attitudes, which in turn gives me the strength to handle any circumstance that can come my way.

Choice and accountability are the two-character traits that separate the strong from the weak. Here are examples of sound character that mature people acknowledge.

1.

MAKING DECISIONS

2.

ACCEPTING THE CONSEQUENCES

3.

BEING RESPONSIBLE FOR YOUR PREFERENCES

The bottom line to choose accountability is that you can no longer blame someone else for the choices you make. As long as the people you associate with are honest and don't manipulate, you have a good chance of being content with your choices. Here is a list of core words with synonyms.

CLEANLINESS

CLEAN BODY
Mind and habits
Personal hygiene and neatness

COURAGE

BRAVERY
BOLDNESS
Daring
Confidence
RESOLVE

EMPATHY

UNDERSTANDING
COMPASSION
Charity
Sensitivity
CONCERN

FORGIVENESS

THE ACT OF LETTING GO OF...

...Past Hurts

...Past Harms

...PAST ILL WILL TOWARDS OTHERS

HONESTY

TRUTHFULNESS

SINCERITY

Honor

Fairness

TRUSTWORTHINESS

Being Genuine

PERSEVERANCE

DEPENDABILITY
Reliability
Responsibility
BEING ORGANIZED
Being punctual
Honoring commitments
PLANNING

"You can't escape the responsibility of tomorrow by evading it today."

ABRAHAM LINCOLN

To grow in your desire to achieve Emotional Sobriety, you will need to lean into the Serenity Prayer. To accept the things, you cannot change. Many of us have belief systems that are the results of challenging childhoods and troubled pasts. I have included quotes from leaders, mentors, and wisdom providers throughout this book. I hope that they give you points of reference and perspective. They certainly have for me.

Often, I would hear my Martial Arts teacher ask, "What do you stand for?" To my surprise, in 1998, I came across a book by the title, What Do You Stand For?, written by Barbara A. Lewis. I realize that her book spoke volumes about the adolescent stage in life. I have re-read her book for what must be the tenth time since then. It has become an essential part of my character. I hope this book and the other authors presented within will help you with your own emotional and physical sobriety.

Spend some time studying healthy and healing words. Practice, just as if you were considering going for a black belt, the ideas, and insights they have to offer, and I believe you will find yourself feeling more content, happy, sober, and becoming your best version of yourself through the process.

Developing positive character traits is not something you do in a vacuum. So much of sobriety is learned through the continuous sharing with those who have walked common paths and faced similar demons. Breaking the isolation that so many people that live in active addiction and realizing that an entire fellowship and community is willing to welcome you in and join you in sobriety is both freeing and eye-opening for most.

The fact that you have reached this far in the book means you want to learn from other people, which certainly sounds like the Seventh Step work to me, and I'm so glad. Continuously stepping out of your comfort zones to learn and practice the twelve and twelve – not alone, but within your self-help community is a huge key to finding not just sobriety – but pure joy.

Are you ready to re-script the "tapes" that have been playing in your head, and practice the healing words that can re-write the rest of your story, and lead a more sober and serene life? Then lean into change. To affirmation. To connection. To shifting from old stories and messages to what is real in the right here and right now.

HEALING, HEALTH, AND PEACE OF MIND ARE AVAILABLE TO ANYONE WILLING TO NOT JUST REACH FOR THEM, BUT PRACTICE WHAT IT TAKES TO EARN THEM.

I wish you emotional sobriety and peace.

I pray that this book when reading again and again, will allow you to grow in a way that you have been seeking.

ABOUT THE AUTHOR

Craig Hutson has an innate capacity to convert his own life experiences into the ability to empathize with others. His father was an episodic alcoholic who had a near-fatal, horrific alcohol-related car accident that could have easily killed him as well as all five of his children. Craig's trauma from this event shaped the then eleven-year-old boy to be determined to be different from his father. Raised in a dysfunctional alcoholic home, Craig struggled to understand the rigidness and ineffective parenting that raised his sense of powerlessness. As an adult, Craig chose to form his understanding of what it meant to be a mature person by embarking on a journey in the Martial Arts, a journey that leads him to develop a strong sense of emotional self-control.

The Martial Arts helped Craig to have the strength and courage to develop a better understanding of how to develop sound character. He experienced a process to understand as an adult what had happened in his formative years. Craig embraced the Martial Arts principles, which enabled himself to achieve Four Master level degrees Arts and a Bachelor of Science Degree in Applied Behavioral Sciences.

Craig's strength today is directly proportional to how weak he was when younger. That strength enables him to have the ability and resolve to accept that people are going to be what and who they are.

Craig has utilized his Bachelor's Degree and Martial Arts Degrees to assist others who have fallen victim to domestic violence and addictions. He worked at the Elgin Community Crisis Center, Advocate Counseling Center and Lutheran Social Services of Illinois.

Craig's journey has enabled him to choose a different path for himself – one which allows him to live in truth and help others to achieve the same. Craig's desire for those reading this book is to get into alignment with their inner self.

TO CONNECT WITH CRAIG OR INVITE HIM TO SPEAK TO YOUR NEXT AUDIENCE, VISIT HIM ONLINE AT:

www.dragonkido.com

OR EMAIL HIM AT:

CraigHutson63@gmail.com

SOURCES CITED

Drop the Rock. Removing Character Defects: Steps Six & Seven → Bill P., Todd W., Sara S. – 2nd ed. 2005. Hazelden Foundation Center City, Minnesota, 55012-0176.

Drop the Rock. The Ripple Effect: Fred H., Hazelden Publishing, Published 2016.

Emotional Sobriety: From Relationship Trauma to Resilience and Balance. Tian Dayton, Ph.D. 1st ed. 2007 Publisher: Health Communications, Inc. 3201 S.W. 15th Street, Deerfield Beach, FL. 33442-8190.

The Soul Mate Secret: Manifest the Love of Your Life with the Law of Attraction. Copyright@2009 by Arielle Ford. Harper Collins Publishers, 10 East 53rd Street, New York, NY 10022.

The Seven Levels of Intimacy: The Art of Loving and the Joy of being loved: Matthew Kelly., Fireside, Rockefeller Center 1230 Avenue of the Americas, New York, NY 10020.

Twelve Steps and Twelve Traditions: General Service Conference-approved Literature: Alcoholics Anonymous World Services, Inc. Box 459, Grand Central Station New York, NY 10163

Alcoholics Anonymous: Fourth Edition, Library of Congress Control Number: 20011094693, ISBN 1-893007-16-2, Printed in the United States of America.

Current Psychotherapies Raymond J. Corsini

You Can't Make Me Angry: Dr. Paul O; 1. Alcoholism -Psychological aspects. 2. Alcoholism - Family relationships.

Twelve-step programs. HV5278; 362.2918; LCCCN: 2002102547 Capizon Publishing, www.capizon.com; Eighth Printing August 2014.

Top 25 Honest Man Quotes https://www.azquotes.com/quotes/topics/honest-man.html

Mission – Dragon Kido http://www.dragonkido.com/mission

Good Reads John Quincy Adams https://www.goodreads.com/quotes/4728-courage-and-perseverance-have-a-magical-talisman-before-which-difficulties

Good Reads Albert Einstein https://www.goodreads.com/quotes/101943-the-intellect-has-little-to-do-on-the-road-to

Good Reads Aristotle https://www.goodreads.com/work/quotes/587647-emotional-intelligence

Psychology Today Magazine https://www.psychologytoday.com/us/blog/emotional-sobriety/201107/what-is-emotional-sobriety

Serenity Prayer https://en.wikipedia.org/wiki/Serenity_Prayer

Fear, The chief activator is http://www.rochrecovery.org/FearsDealingWith1.html

Self-Respect Quotes C.N. Douglas https://www.bartleby.com/348/1208.html

Peacock Wildlife Way Station, https://wildlifewaystation.org/animals/species/peacock

Abraham Lincoln https://www.sermoncentral.com/sermon-illustrations/48547/you-can-t-escape-the-responsibility-of- tomorrow-by-sermon central

Jonathan Edwards, https://www.christianquotes.info/quotes-by-topic/quotes-about-jealousy/

John Homer Miller https://www.goodreads.com/quotes/173270-circumstances-and-situations-do-color-life-but-you-have-been

American Heritage Dictionary; Published 1969; Author, American Heritage Publishing Company.

Printed in Great Britain
by Amazon